SAVING ANIMALS FROM THE BRINK

A SCARY PREDICTION

BISON COMEBACK

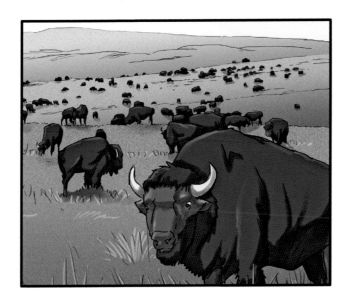

BY TIM COOKE
ILLUSTRATED BY ALESSANDRO VALDRIGHI

BEARPORT PUBLISHING
Minneapolis, Minnesota

BEAR CLAW

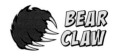

Credits: 20, © Inger Eriksen/Shutterstock; 21, © Mikadun/Shutterstock; 22t, © Smithy55/
Shutterstock; 22b, © Lisa Banfield/Shutterstock.

Editor: Sarah Eason
Proofreader: Harriet McGregor
Designers: Jessica Moon and Steve Mead
Picture Researcher: Rachel Blount

DISCLAIMER: This graphic story is a dramatization based on true events. It is intended to give the reader a sense of the narrative rather than a presentation of actual details as they occurred.

Library of Congress Cataloging-in-Publication Data

Names: Cooke, Tim, 1961- author. | Valdrighi, Alessandro, illustrator.
Title: A scary prediction : bison comeback / by Tim Cooke ; illustrated by
    Alessandro Valdrighi.
Description: Bear claw books edition. | Minneapolis, Minnesota : Bearport
    Publishing Company, [2022] | Series: Saving animals from the brink |
    Includes bibliographical references and index.
Identifiers: LCCN 2020058595 (print) | LCCN 2020058596 (ebook) | ISBN
    9781636910444 (library binding) | ISBN 9781636910512 (paperback) | ISBN
    9781636910581 (ebook)
Subjects: LCSH: Hornaday, William T. (William Temple), 1854-1937--Juvenile
    literature. | American bison--Conservation--United States--Juvenile
    literature. | Endangered species--Conservation--United States--Juvenile
    literature.
Classification: LCC QL737.U53 C659 2022 (print) | LCC QL737.U53 (ebook) |
    DDC 599.64/3--dc23
LC record available at https://lccn.loc.gov/2020058595
LC ebook record available at https://lccn.loc.gov/2020058596

For more information, write to Bearport Publishing, 5357 Penn Avenue South, Minneapolis, MN 55419. Printed in the United States of America.

CONTENTS

CHAPTER 1

DISASTER!

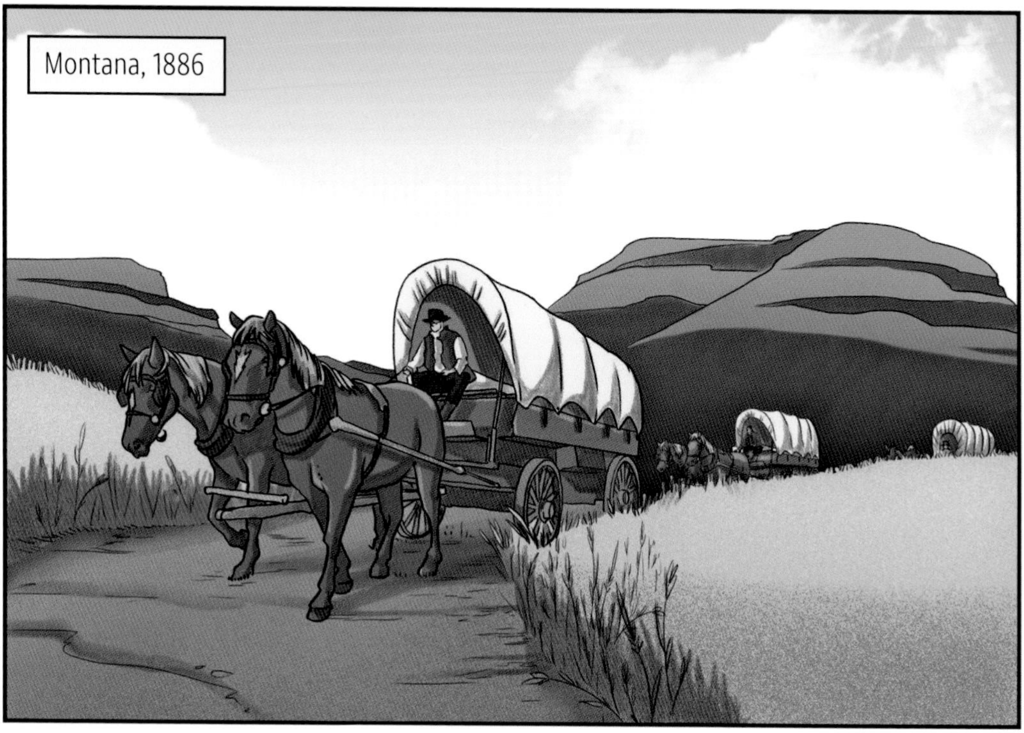
Montana, 1886

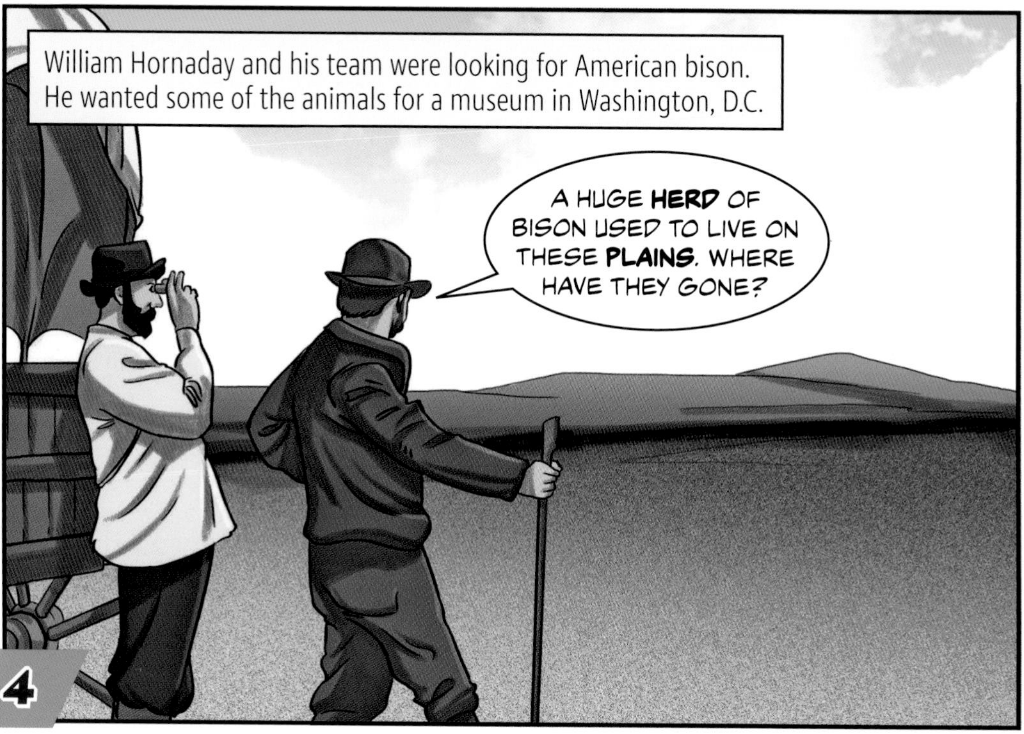
William Hornaday and his team were looking for American bison. He wanted some of the animals for a museum in Washington, D.C.
A HUGE **HERD** OF BISON USED TO LIVE ON THESE **PLAINS**. WHERE HAVE THEY GONE?

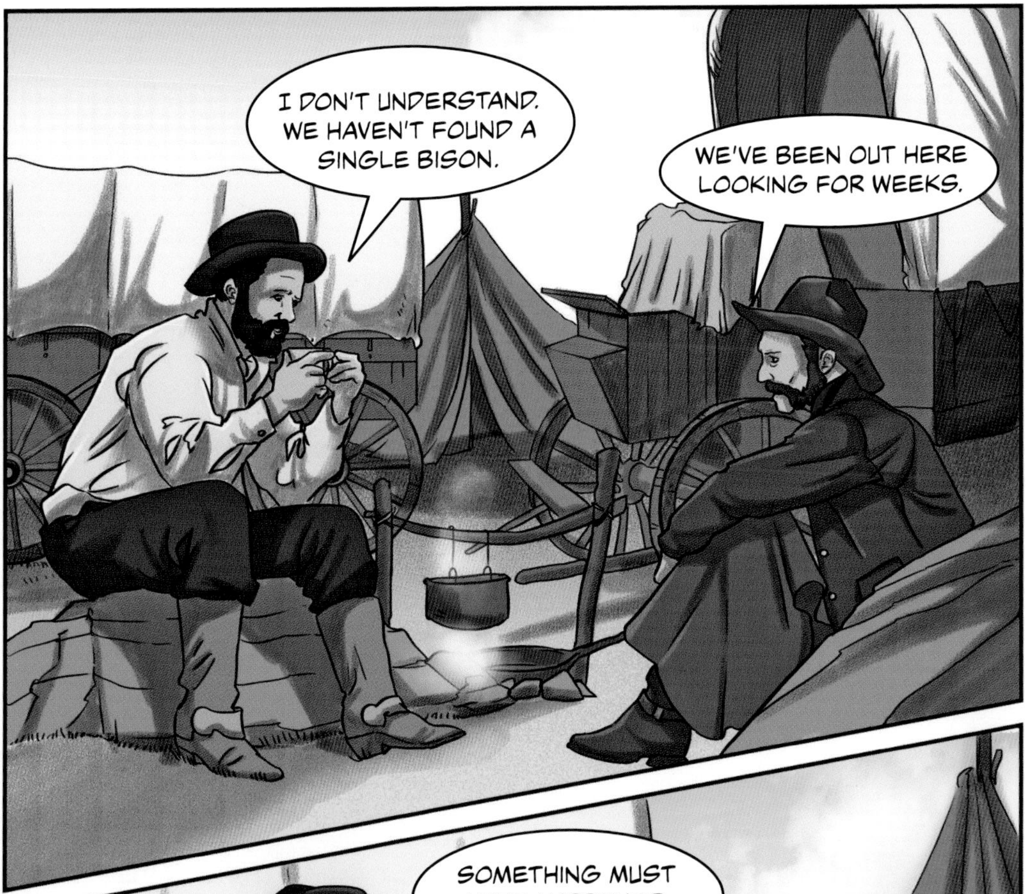
I DON'T UNDERSTAND. WE HAVEN'T FOUND A SINGLE BISON.
WE'VE BEEN OUT HERE LOOKING FOR WEEKS.

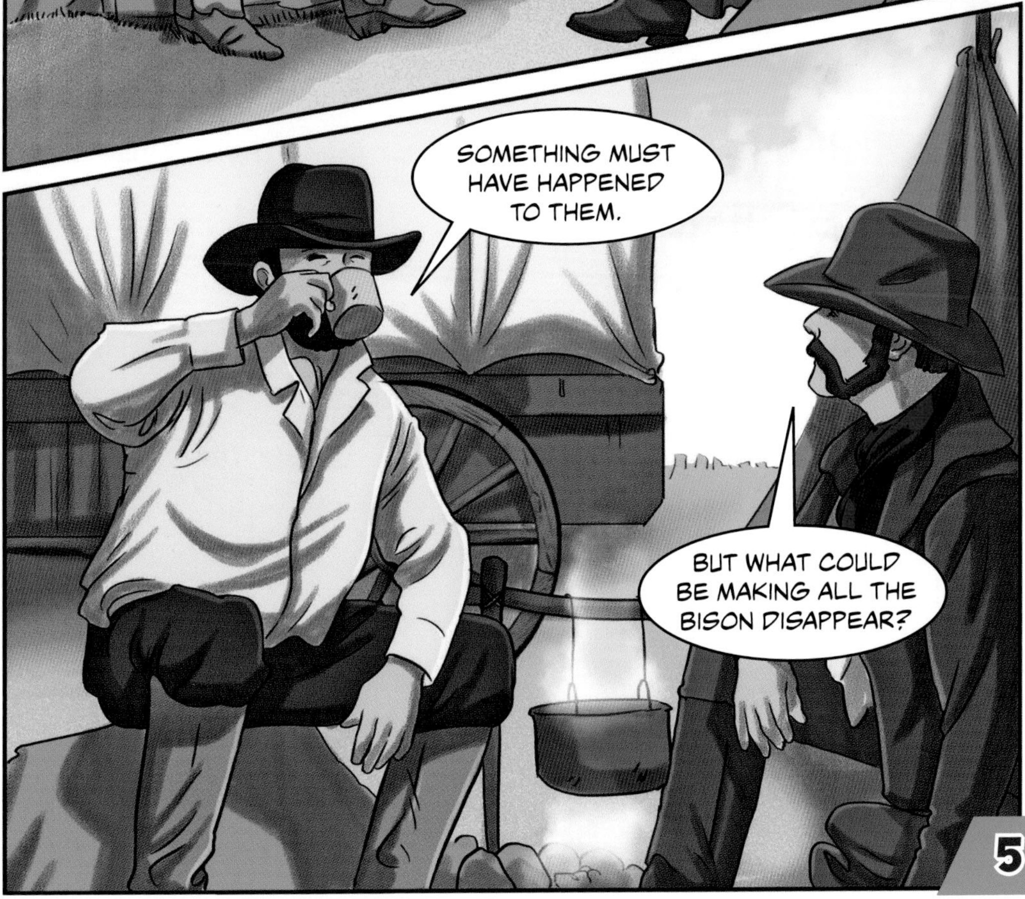
SOMETHING MUST HAVE HAPPENED TO THEM.
BUT WHAT COULD BE MAKING ALL THE BISON DISAPPEAR?

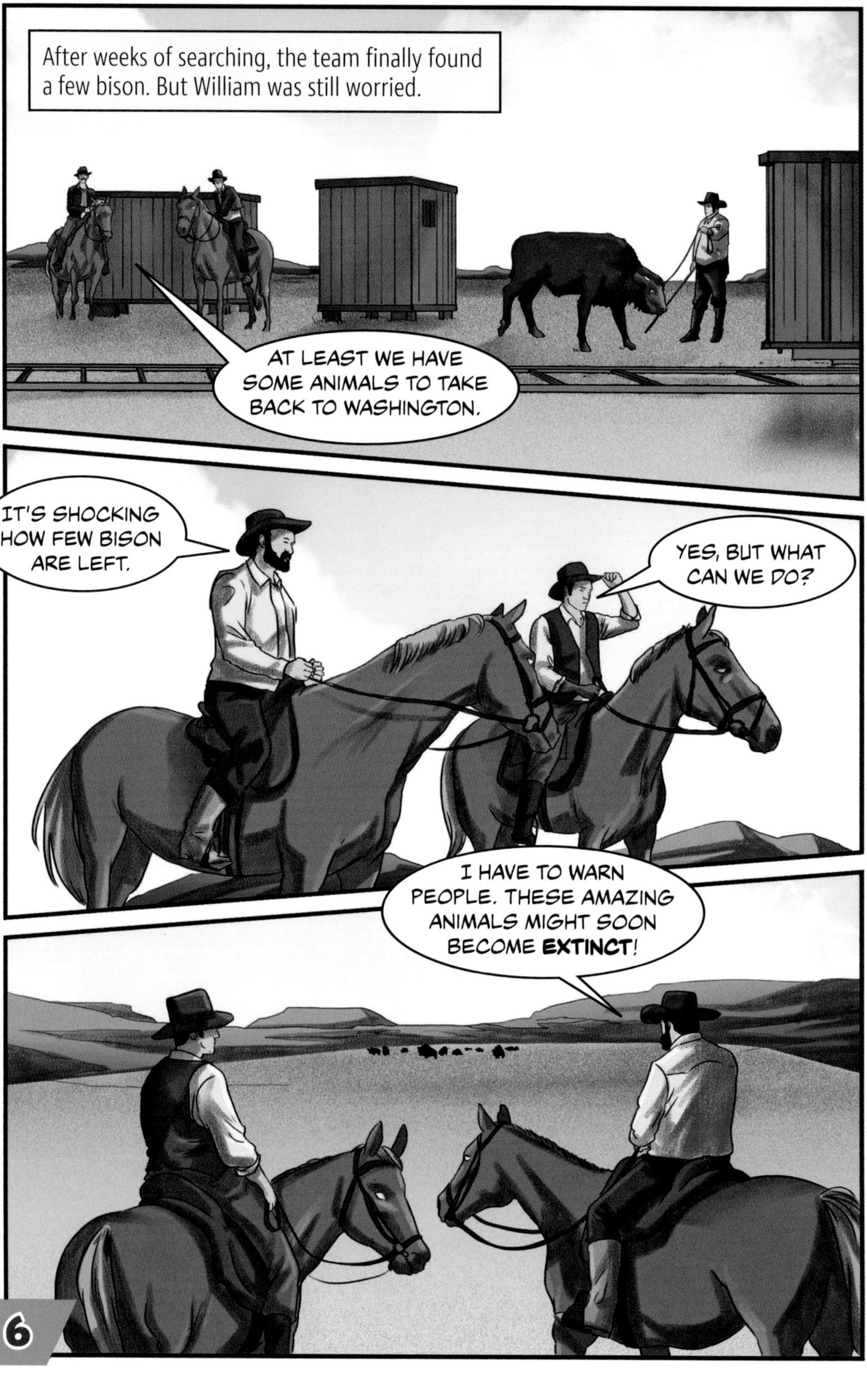
After weeks of searching, the team finally found a few bison. But William was still worried.
AT LEAST WE HAVE SOME ANIMALS TO TAKE BACK TO WASHINGTON.
IT'S SHOCKING HOW FEW BISON ARE LEFT.
YES, BUT WHAT CAN WE DO?
I HAVE TO WARN PEOPLE. THESE AMAZING ANIMALS MIGHT SOON BECOME **EXTINCT**!

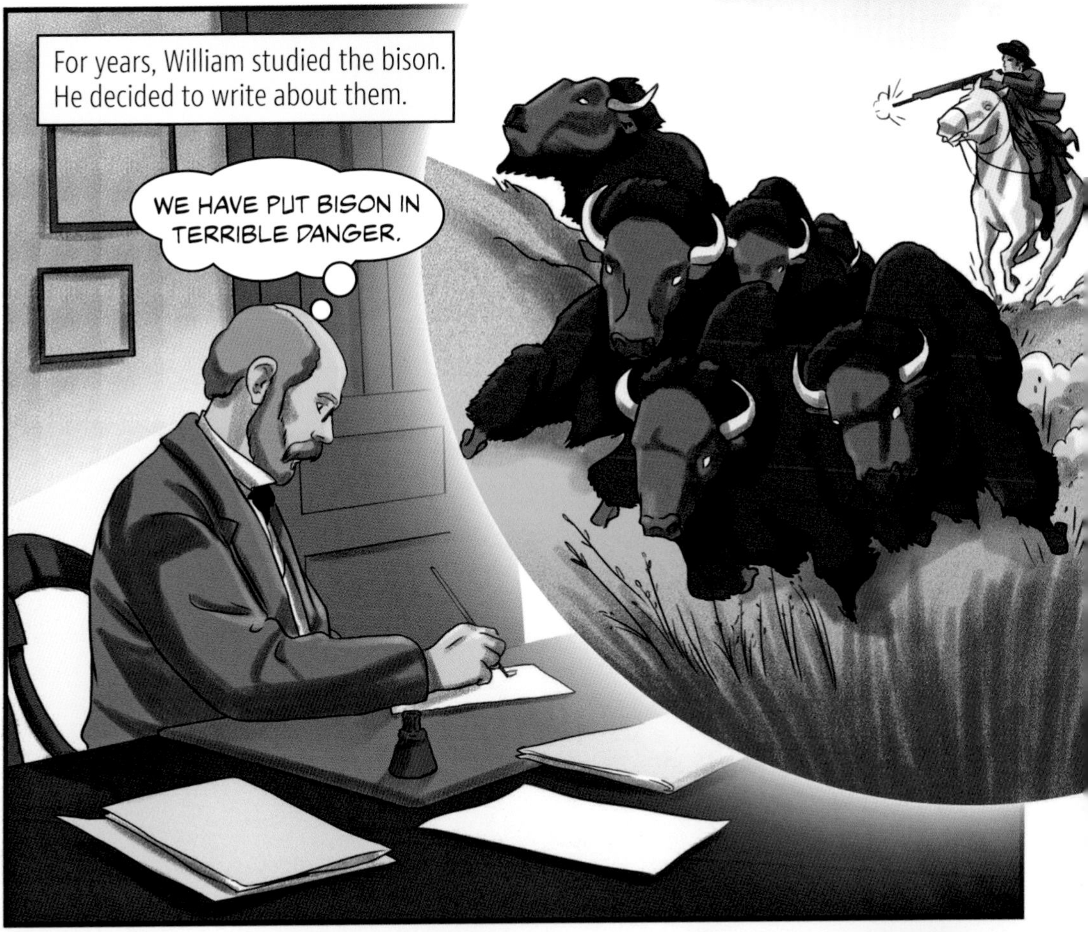
For years, William studied the bison. He decided to write about them.
WE HAVE PUT BISON IN TERRIBLE DANGER.

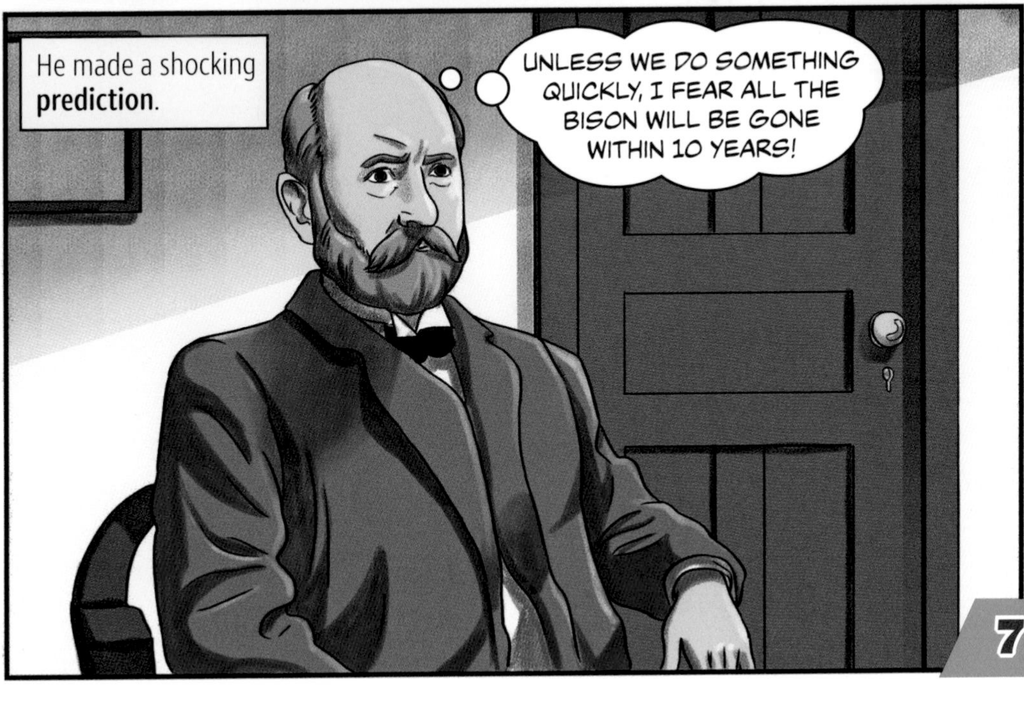
He made a shocking **prediction**.
UNLESS WE DO SOMETHING QUICKLY, I FEAR ALL THE BISON WILL BE GONE WITHIN 10 YEARS!

CHAPTER 2

SAVING THE BISON

At one time, as many as 30 to 60 million bison roamed the plains of North America.

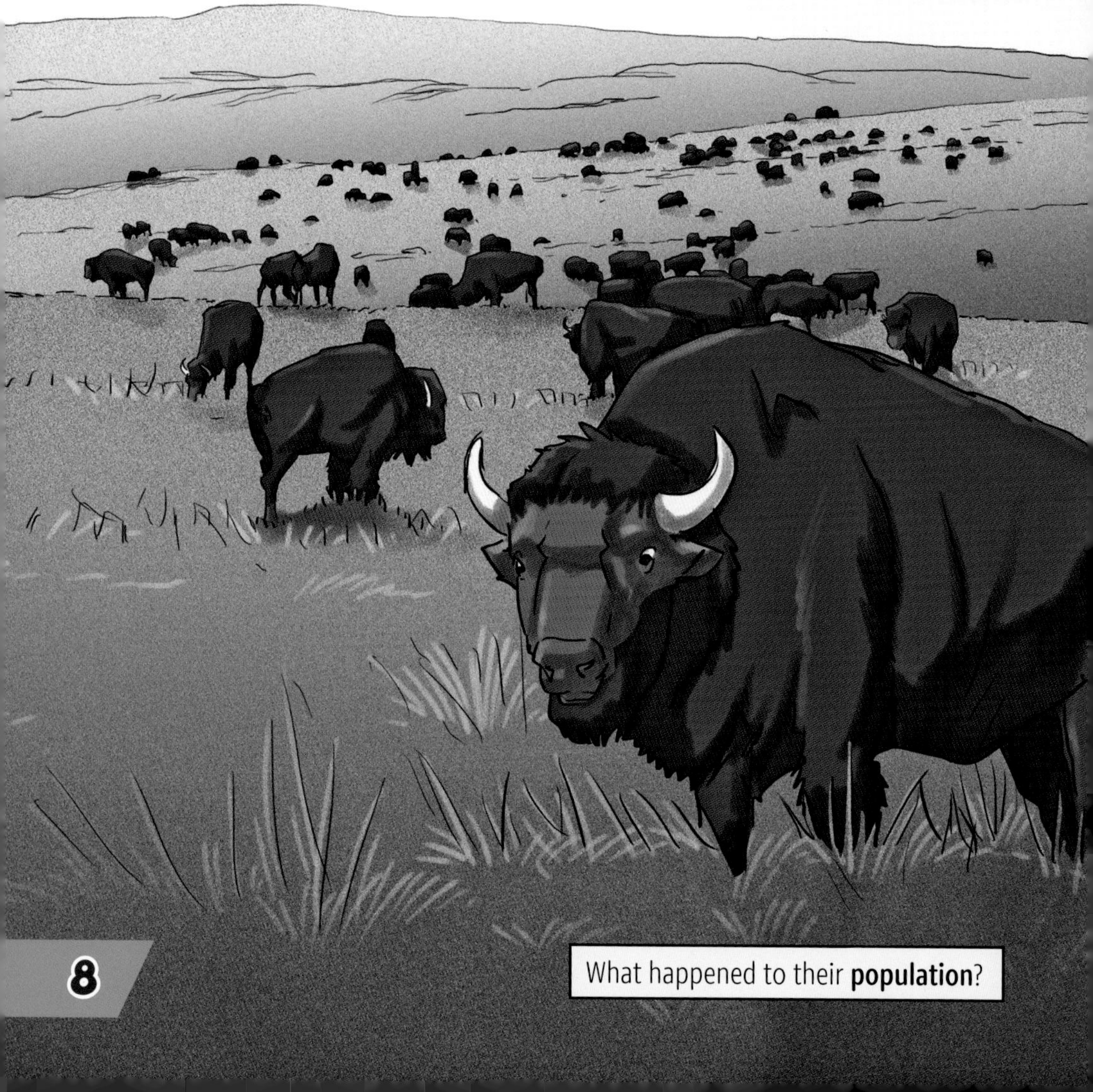
What happened to their **population**?

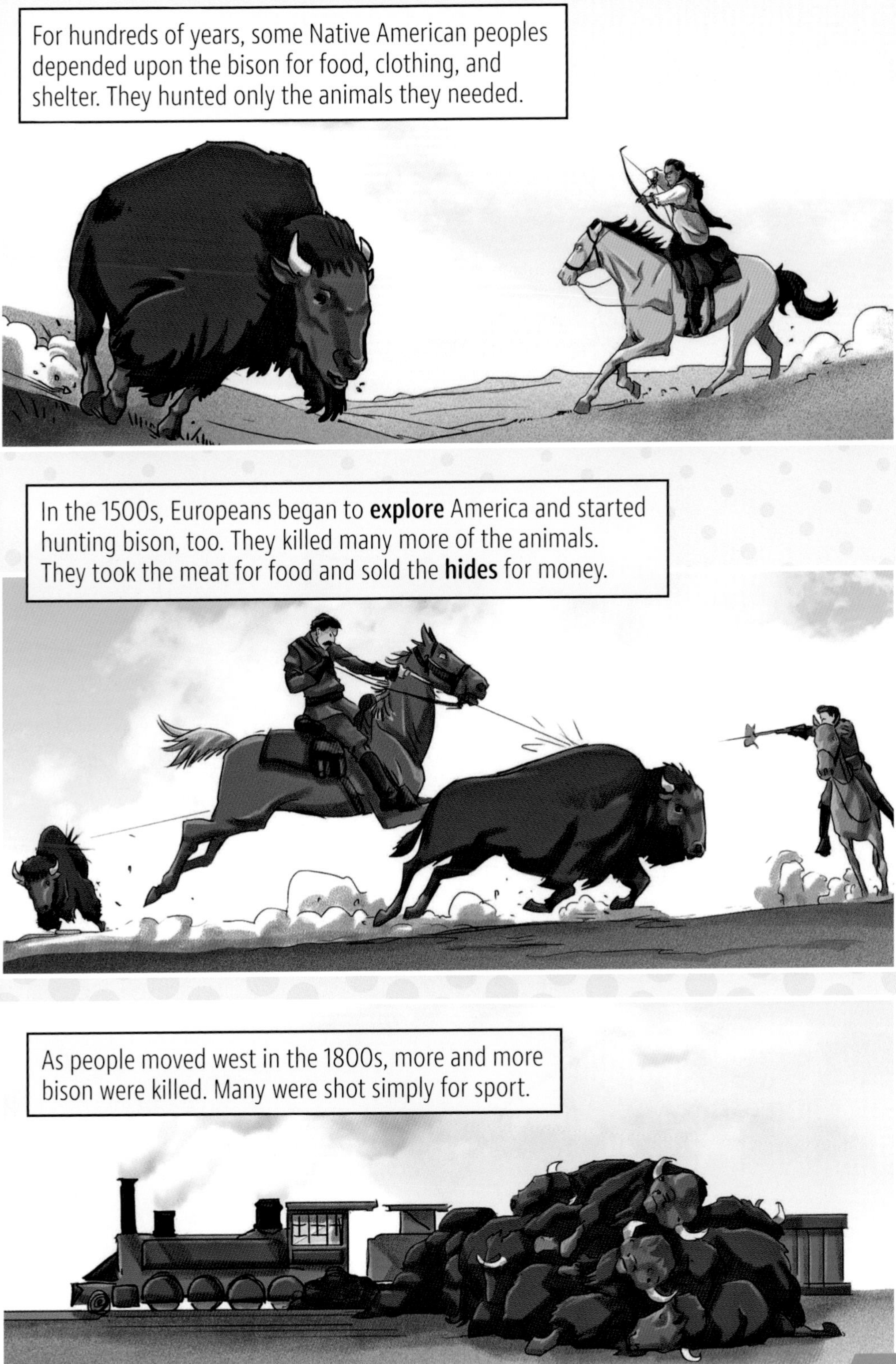
For hundreds of years, some Native American peoples depended upon the bison for food, clothing, and shelter. They hunted only the animals they needed.
In the 1500s, Europeans began to explore America and started hunting bison, too. They killed many more of the animals. They took the meat for food and sold the hides for money.
As people moved west in the 1800s, more and more bison were killed. Many were shot simply for sport.

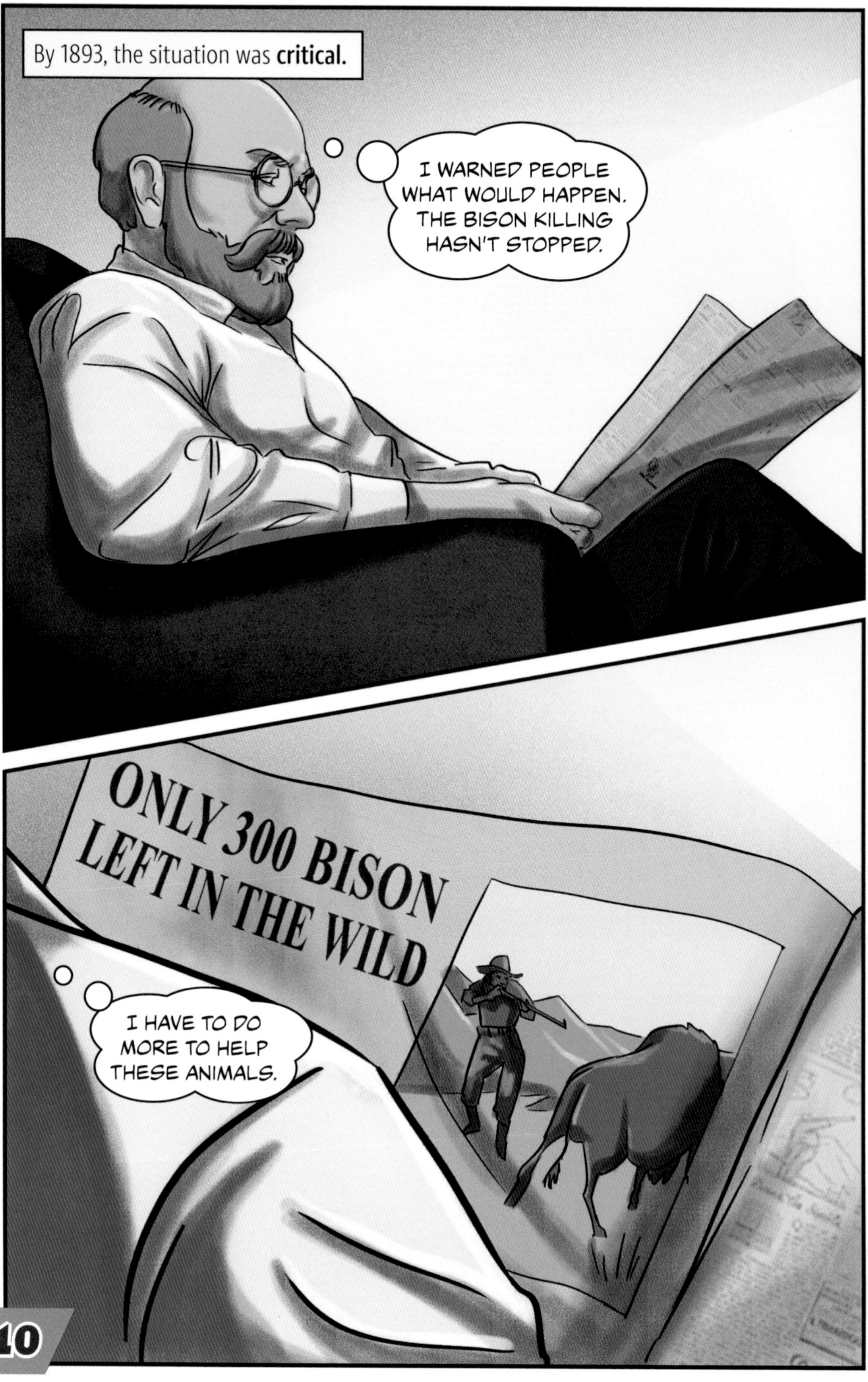
By 1893, the situation was **critical.**
I WARNED PEOPLE WHAT WOULD HAPPEN. THE BISON KILLING HASN'T STOPPED.
ONLY 300 BISON LEFT IN THE WILD
I HAVE TO DO MORE TO HELP THESE ANIMALS.

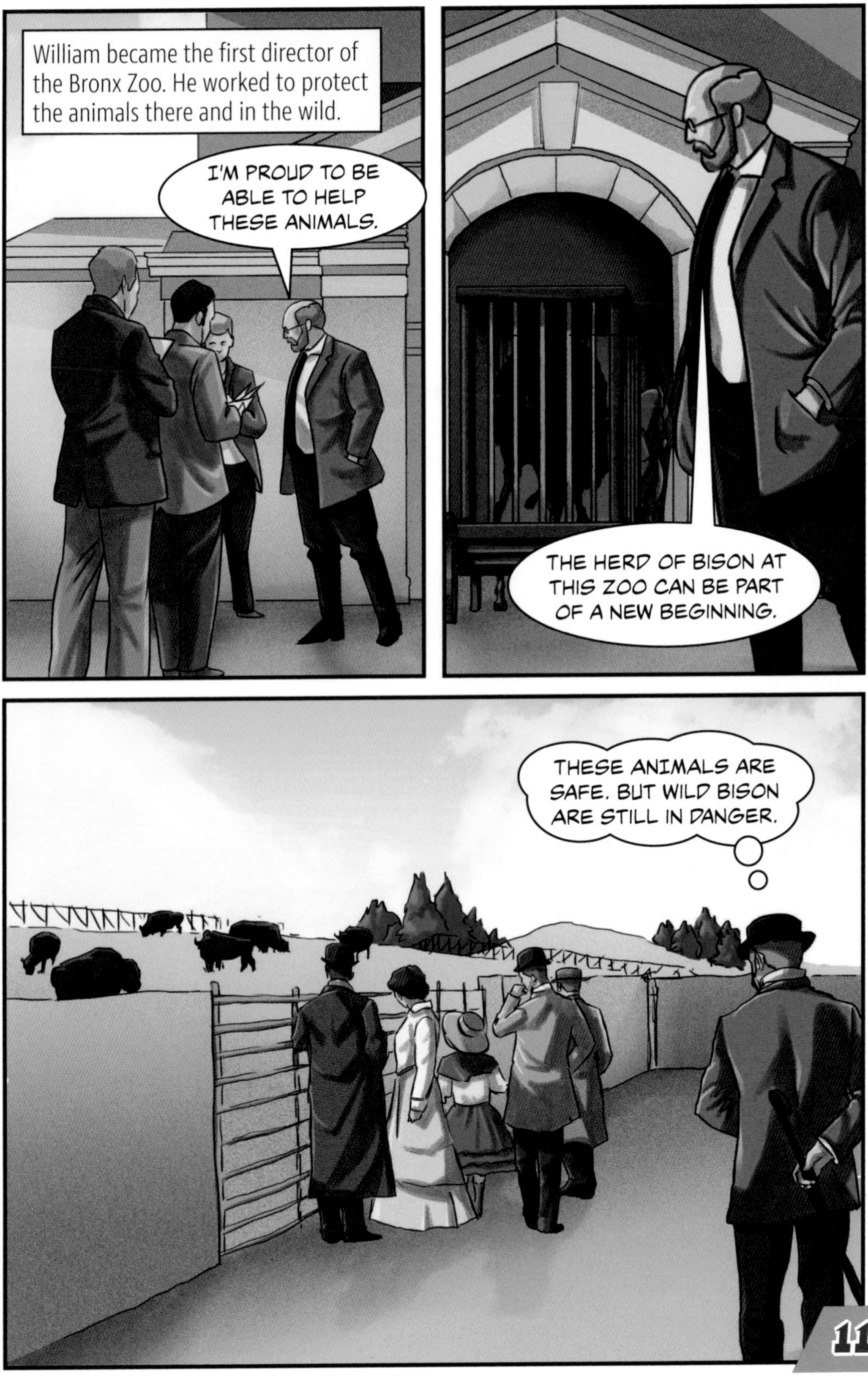
William became the first director of the Bronx Zoo. He worked to protect the animals there and in the wild.
I'M PROUD TO BE ABLE TO HELP THESE ANIMALS.
THE HERD OF BISON AT THIS ZOO CAN BE PART OF A NEW BEGINNING.
THESE ANIMALS ARE SAFE. BUT WILD BISON ARE STILL IN DANGER.

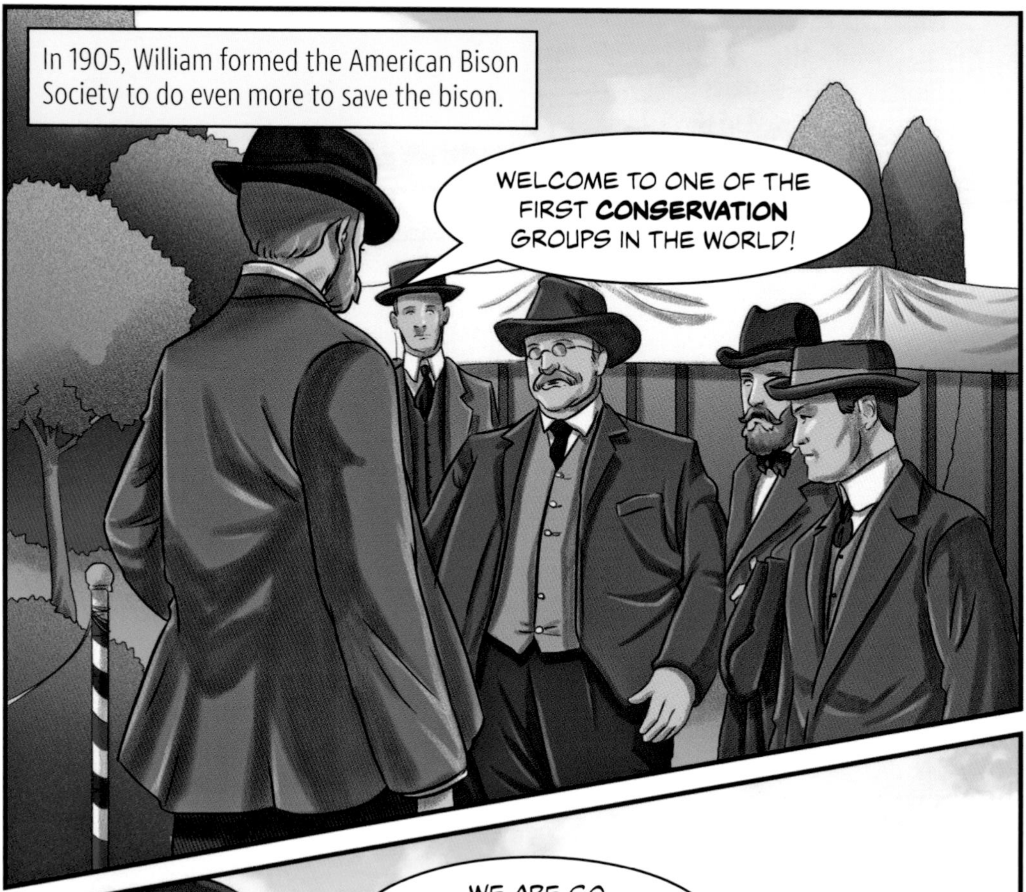
In 1905, William formed the American Bison Society to do even more to save the bison.
WELCOME TO ONE OF THE FIRST **CONSERVATION** GROUPS IN THE WORLD!

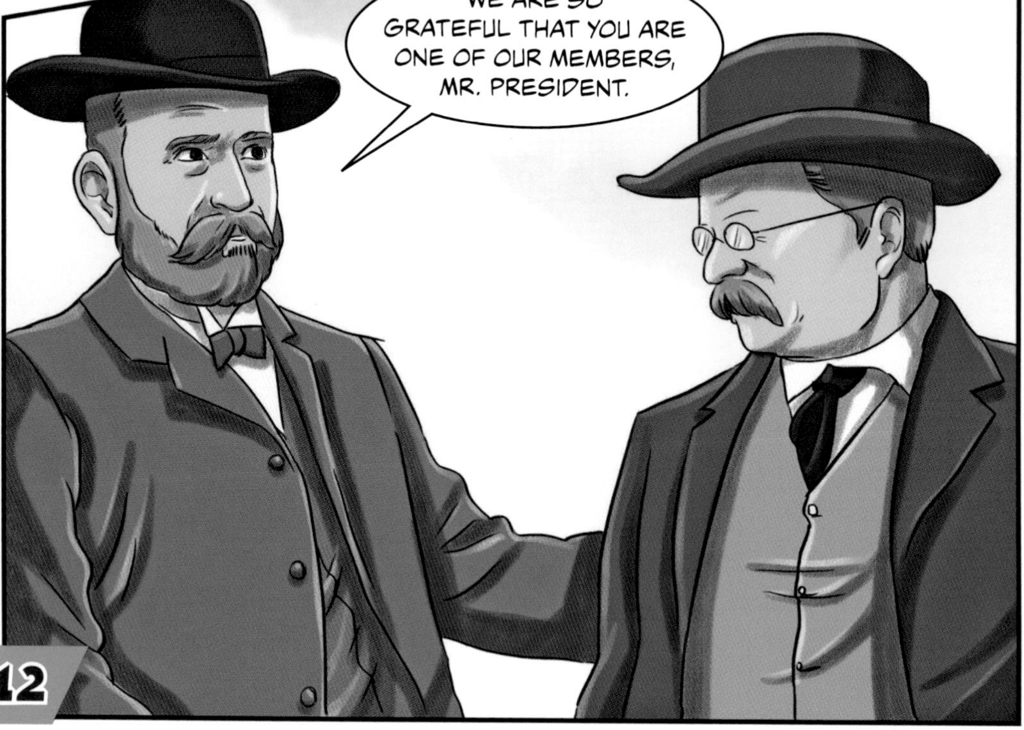
WE ARE SO GRATEFUL THAT YOU ARE ONE OF OUR MEMBERS, MR. PRESIDENT.

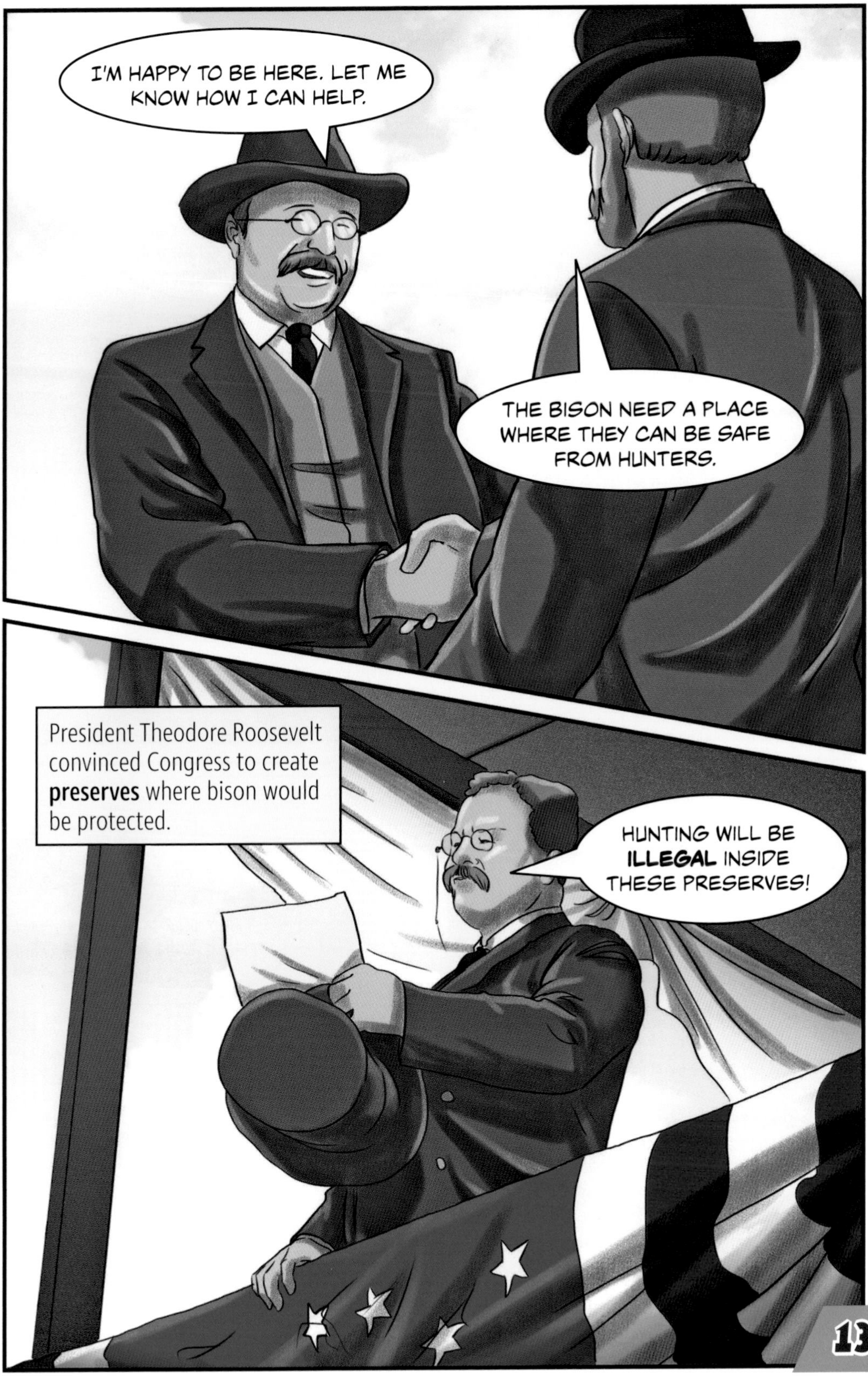
I'M HAPPY TO BE HERE. LET ME KNOW HOW I CAN HELP.
THE BISON NEED A PLACE WHERE THEY CAN BE SAFE FROM HUNTERS.
President Theodore Roosevelt convinced Congress to create **preserves** where bison would be protected.
HUNTING WILL BE **ILLEGAL** INSIDE THESE PRESERVES!

CHAPTER 3

PROTECTING THE BISON

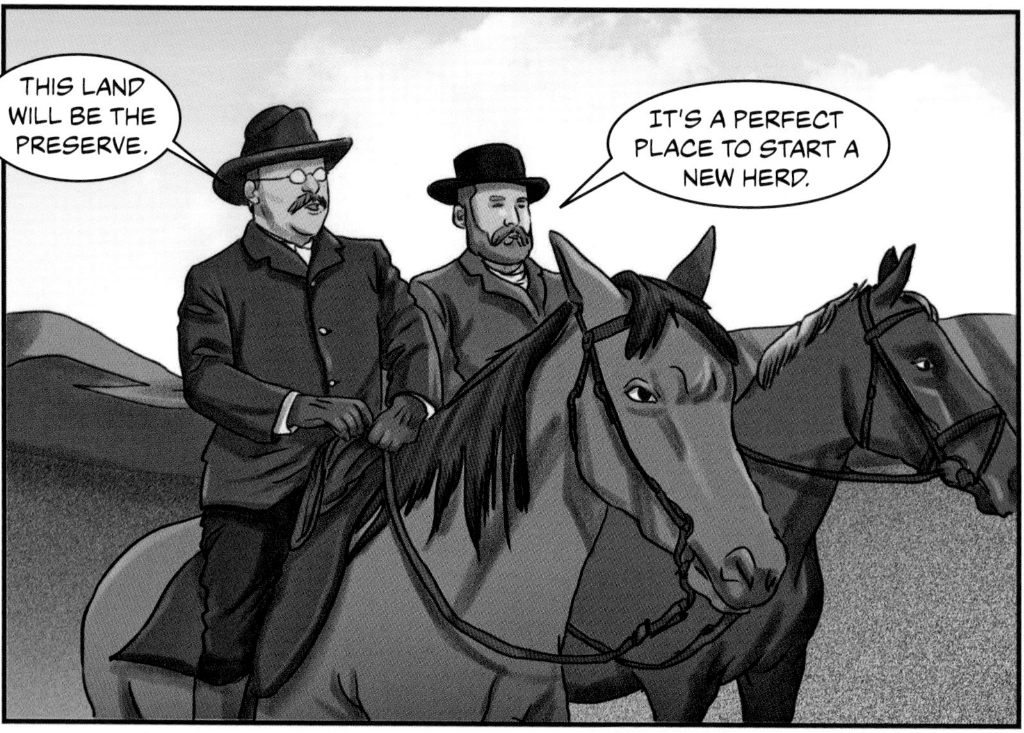
THIS LAND WILL BE THE PRESERVE.
IT'S A PERFECT PLACE TO START A NEW HERD.

With a safe place for the bison to live, William arranged for 15 bison to be brought to Oklahoma from the zoo in New York City.

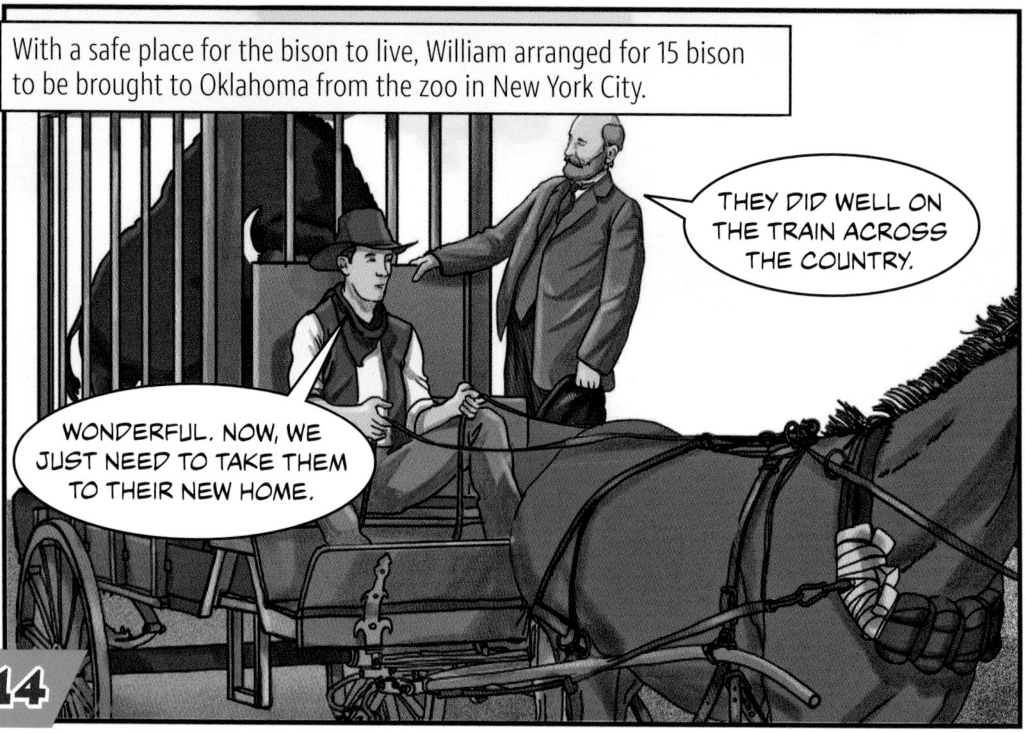
THEY DID WELL ON THE TRAIN ACROSS THE COUNTRY.
WONDERFUL. NOW, WE JUST NEED TO TAKE THEM TO THEIR NEW HOME.

Several years later, the bison herd had more than doubled in size.

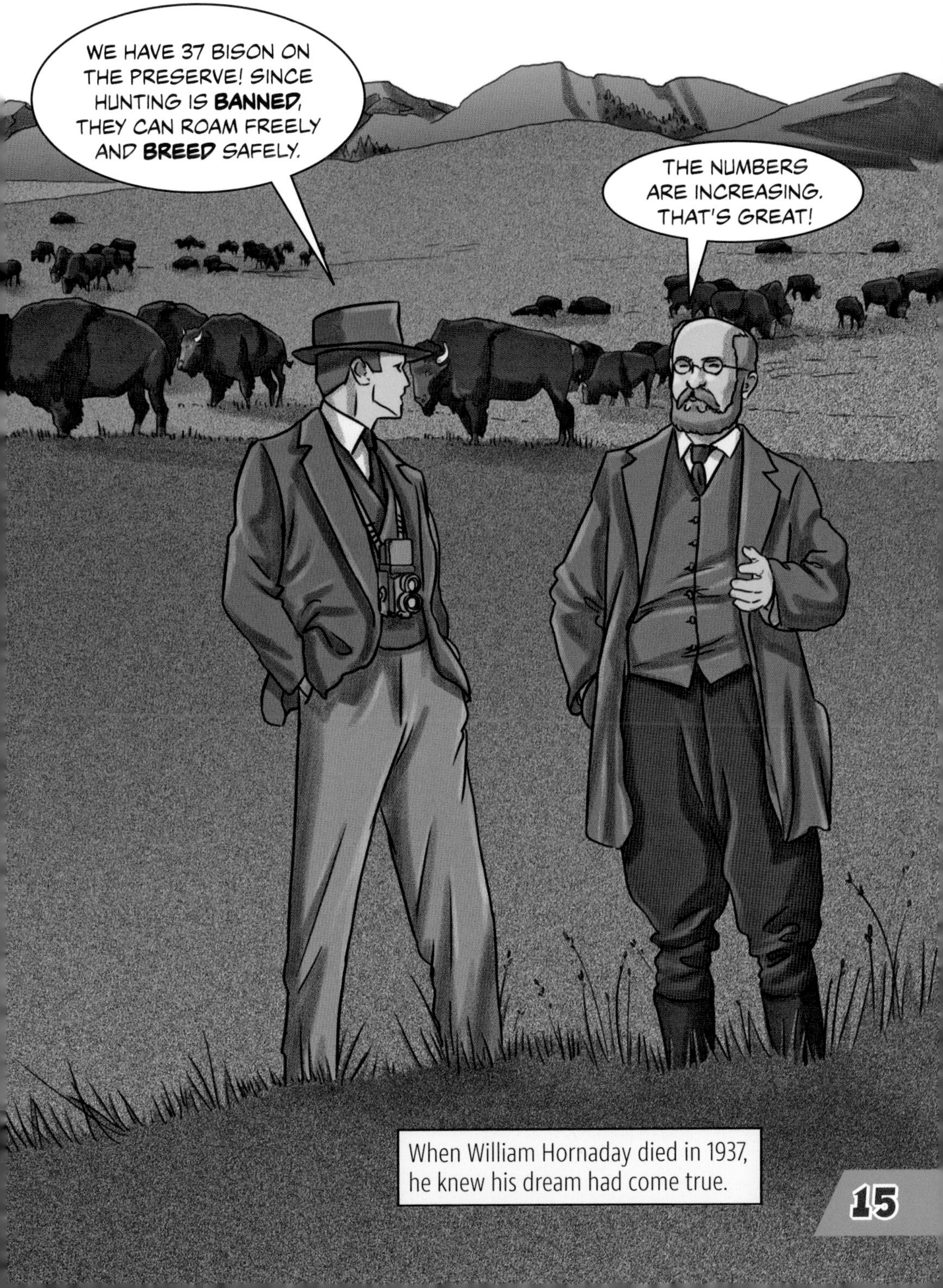
WE HAVE 37 BISON ON THE PRESERVE! SINCE HUNTING IS **BANNED**, THEY CAN ROAM FREELY AND **BREED** SAFELY.
THE NUMBERS ARE INCREASING. THAT'S GREAT!
When William Hornaday died in 1937, he knew his dream had come true.

Most of the bison found in the western United States are direct **descendants** of William's bison from the Bronx Zoo.

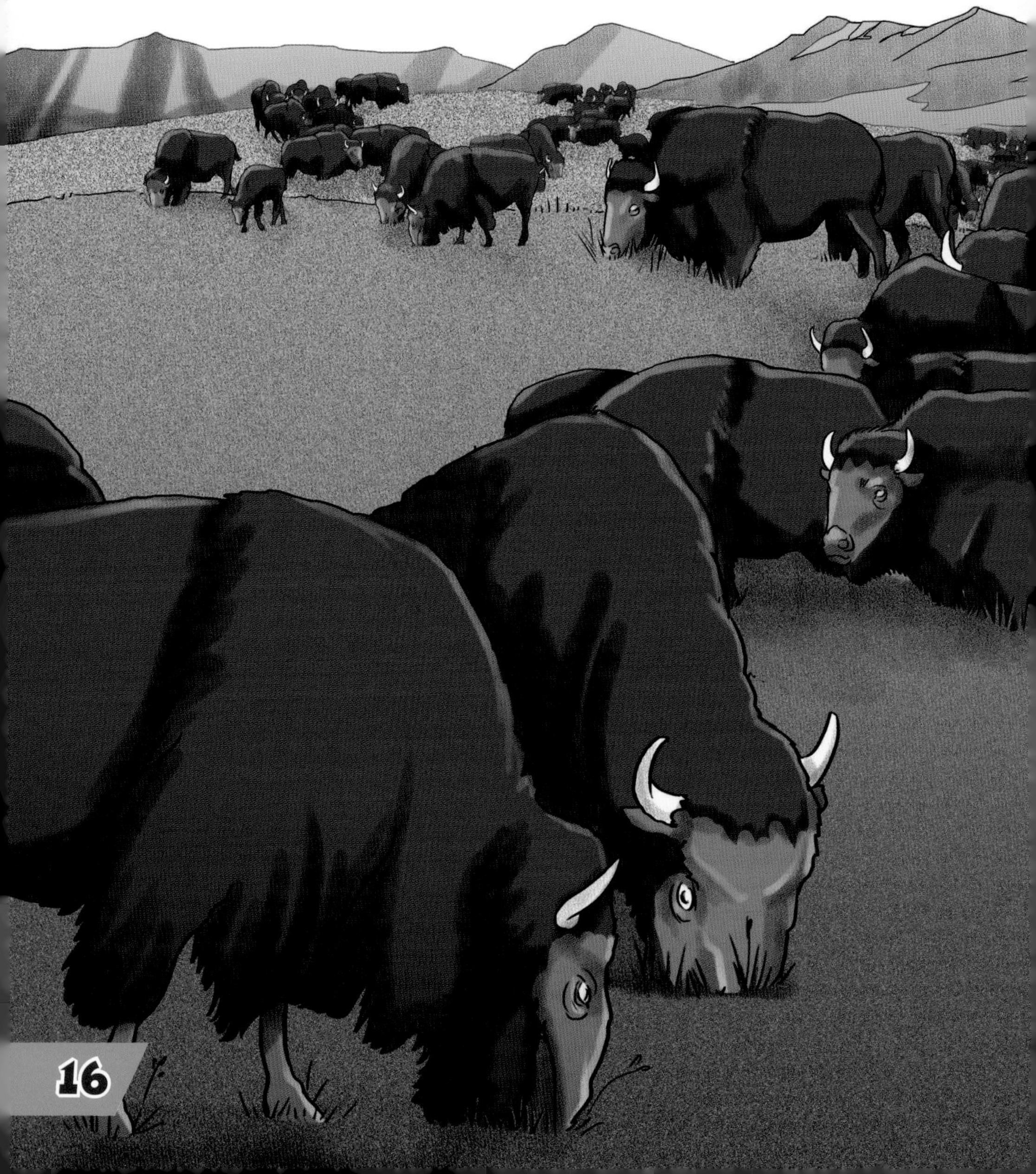

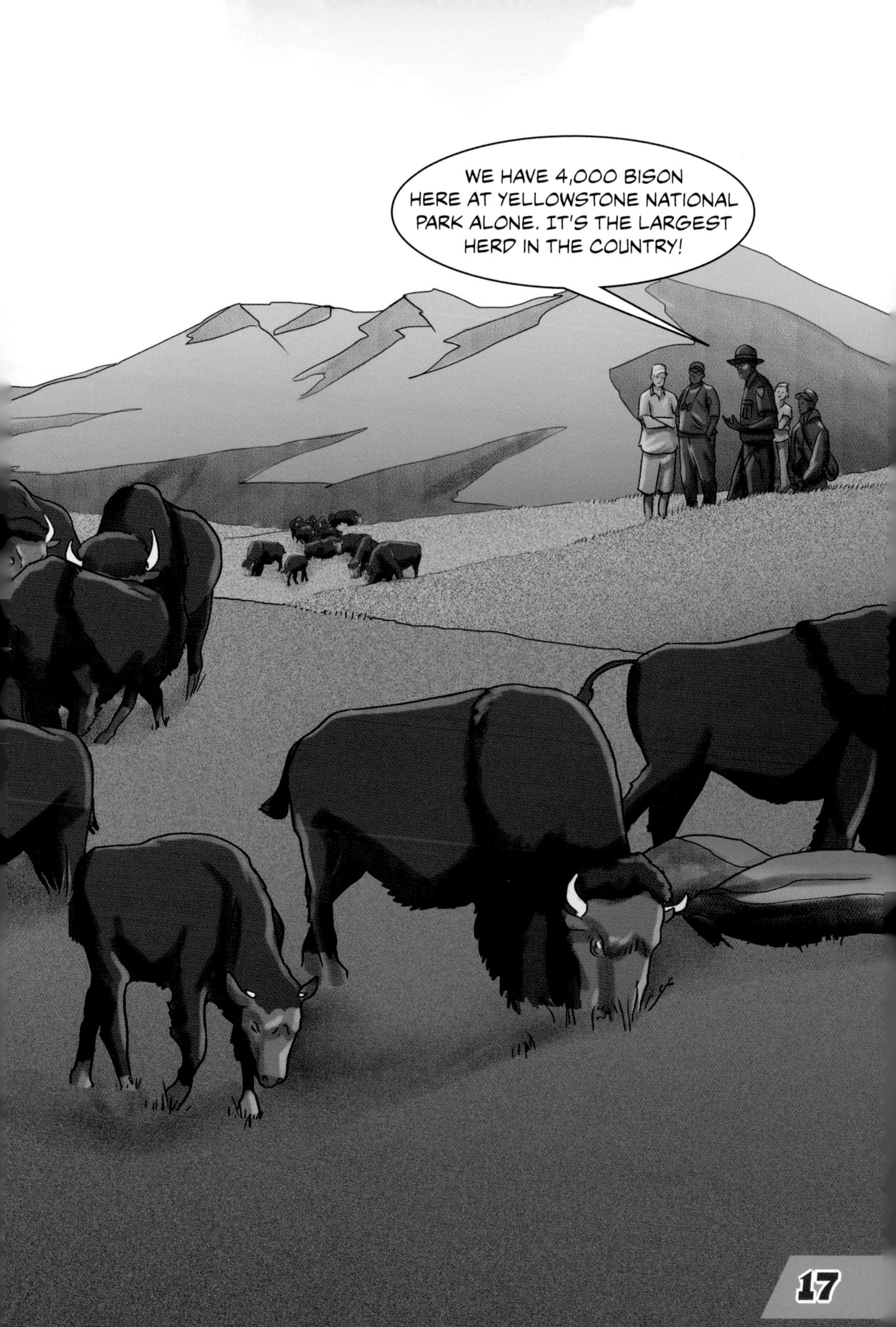
WE HAVE 4,000 BISON HERE AT YELLOWSTONE NATIONAL PARK ALONE. IT'S THE LARGEST HERD IN THE COUNTRY!

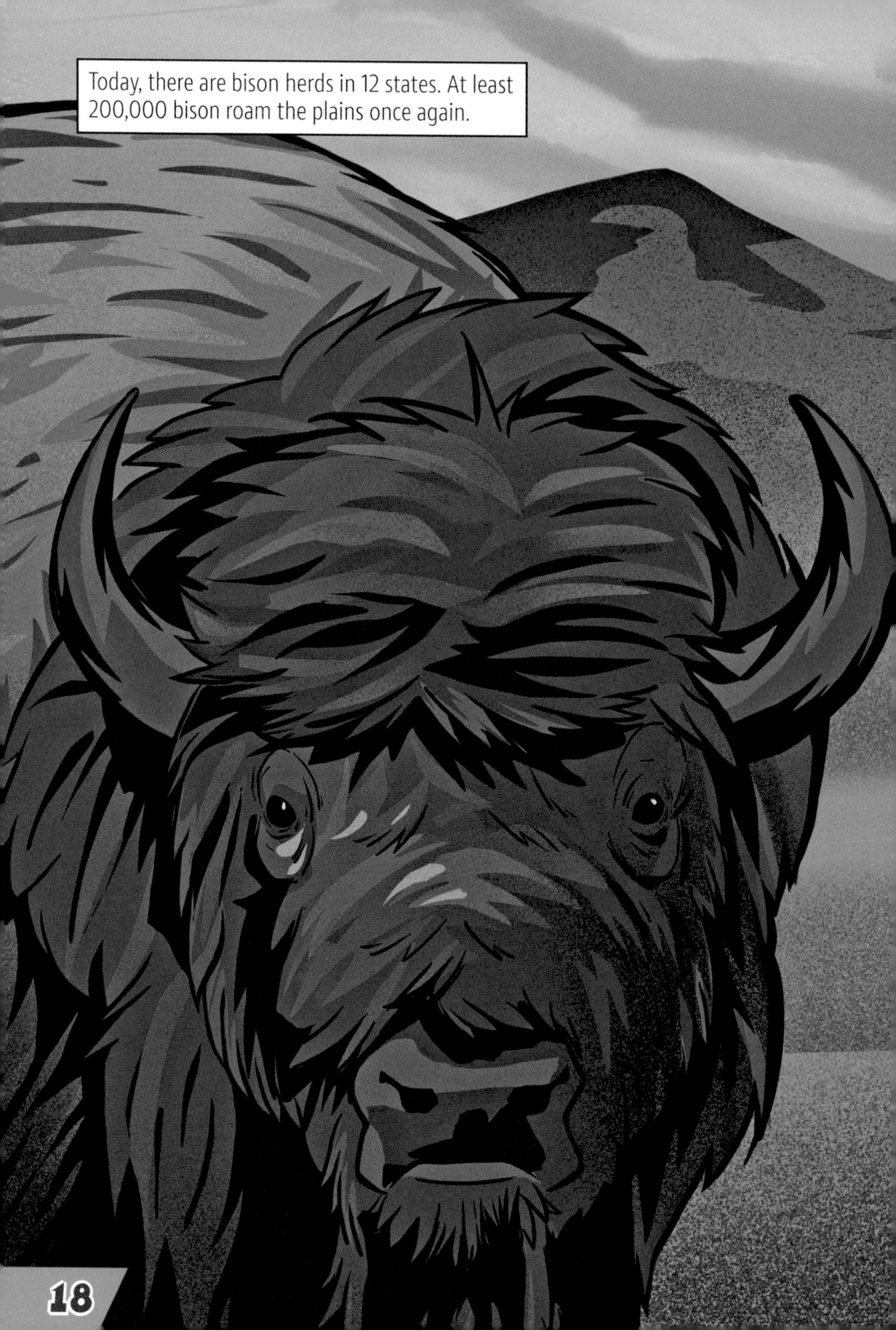
Today, there are bison herds in 12 states. At least 200,000 bison roam the plains once again.

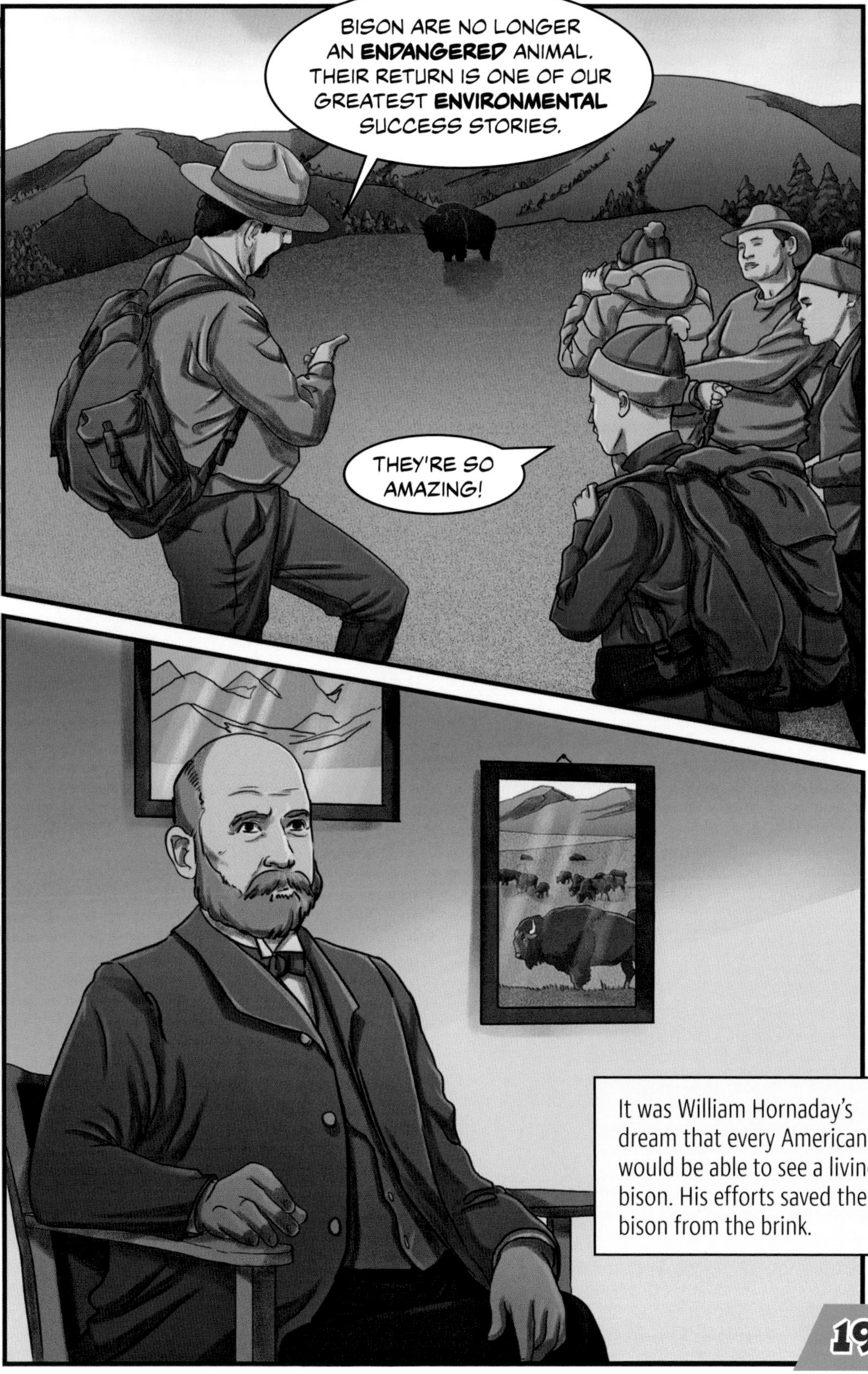
BISON ARE NO LONGER AN **ENDANGERED** ANIMAL. THEIR RETURN IS ONE OF OUR GREATEST **ENVIRONMENTAL** SUCCESS STORIES.
THEY'RE SO AMAZING!
It was William Hornaday's dream that every American would be able to see a living bison. His efforts saved the bison from the brink.

BISON FACTS

In 1973, Congress passed the Endangered Species Act. This law protects animals and plants that are in danger of dying out. Hunting, capturing, harming, or collecting endangered species is illegal under this law.

Environmentalists have asked the U.S. government to list the American bison under the Endangered Species Act. This would give the bison more protection.

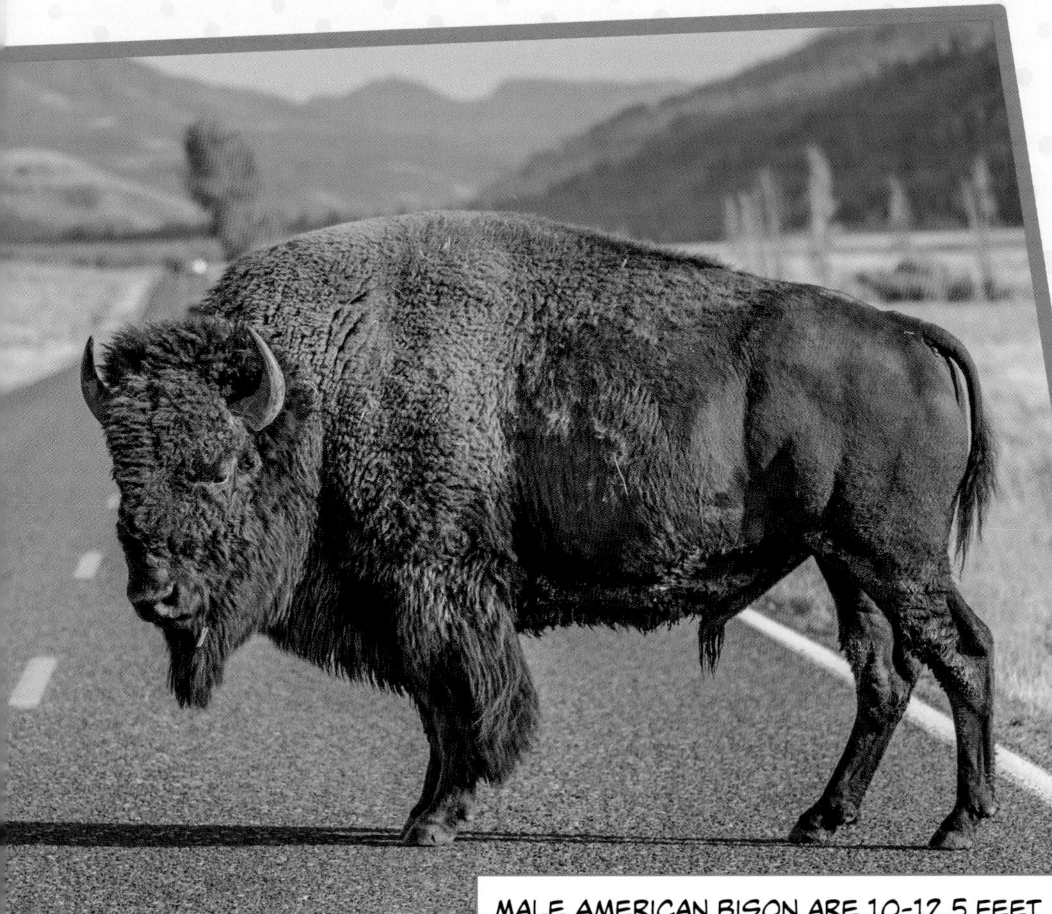

MALE AMERICAN BISON ARE 10-12.5 FEET (3-4 M) LONG AND UP TO 6 FT (1.8 M) TALL. FEMALES ARE SLIGHTLY SMALLER.

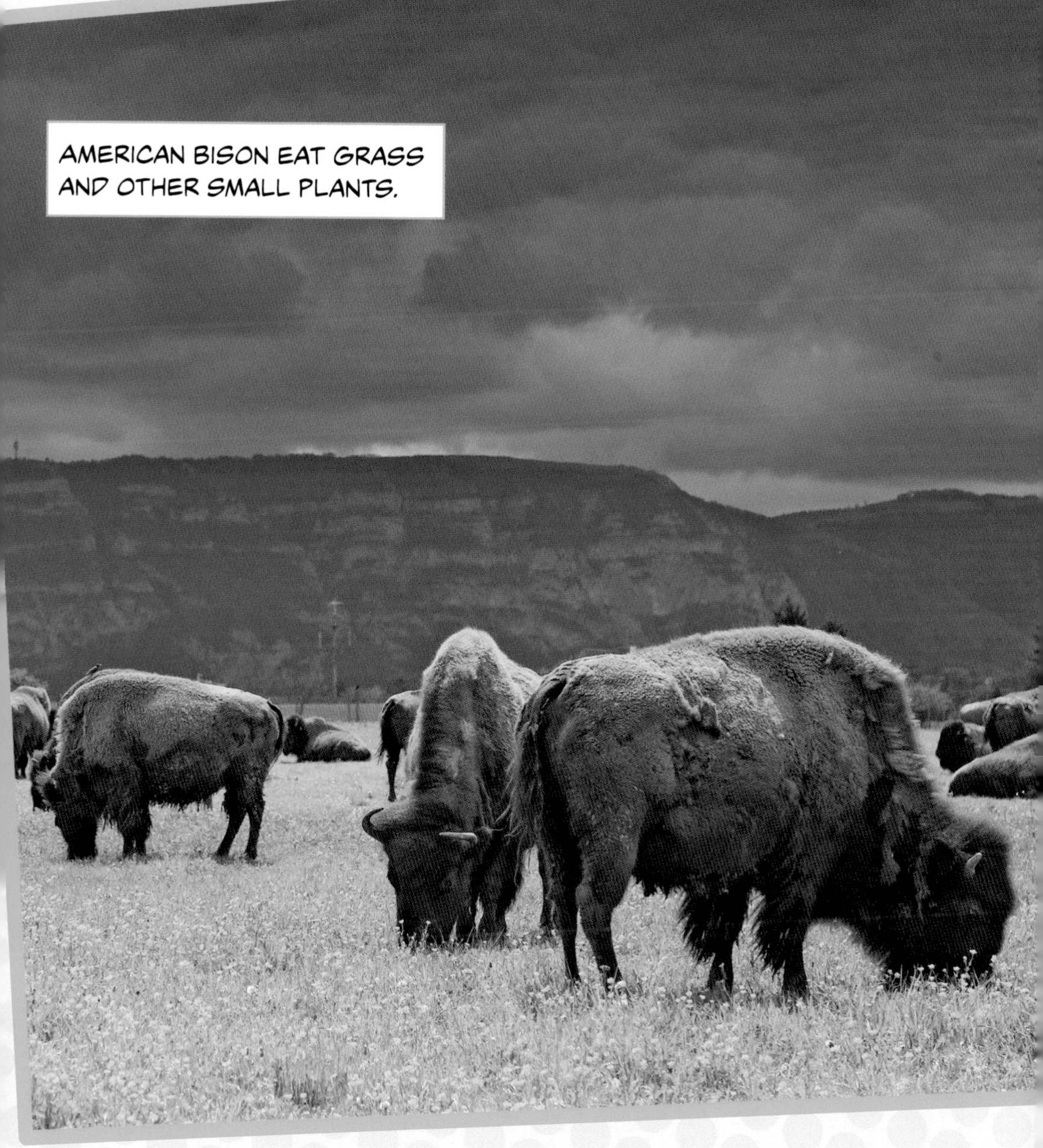
AMERICAN BISON EAT GRASS AND OTHER SMALL PLANTS.

Although William Hornaday saved the bison from extinction, there are still fewer bison today than there were in the past. Before the 1800s, there were about 30–60 million bison in North America. Today, there are about 200,000–450,000 bison on ranches and about 20,000 on preserves and in parks.

OTHER ANIMALS IN DANGER

The American bison is making a comeback, but other similar animals are still struggling.

CUVIER'S GAZELLE

There are fewer than 2,500 Cuvier's (KYOO-vee-ayz) gazelles in the world. These animals live in the African countries of Algeria, Morocco, and Tunisia. They are threatened by the loss of their **habitat**. Fourteen African countries are working together to protect the gazelles and other endangered animals.

CUVIER'S GAZELLES BORN IN ZOOS HAVE BEEN RELEASED IN THE WILD IN TUNISIA.

THERE ARE FEWER THAN 2,500 WESTERN GIANT ELANDS IN THE WORLD.

WESTERN GIANT ELAND

The western giant eland is a type of antelope. It is one of the largest antelopes in Africa. The animal is in danger because of hunting and because its habitat is being destroyed. African countries, such as Guinea and Mali, have passed laws to protect the western giant eland.

GLOSSARY

banned not allowed

breed to produce young

conservation the protection of wildlife and nature

critical very serious

descendants people or animals that come from a family that lived earlier in time

endangered in danger of dying out

environmental related to the land, air, and sea; environmentalists are people who work to protect the land, plants, and animals

explore to travel into a new area to find out about it

extinct died out

habitat where a plant or animal normally lives

herd a large group of animals

hides the skins of animals

illegal against the law

plains open grasslands in North America

population the total number of a kind of animal living in a place

prediction a thought about what is going to happen in the future

preserves protected areas of land set aside for animals or plants

INDEX

READ MORE

Grunbaum, Mara. *Bison (Nature's Children)*. New York: Children's Press, 2019.

Kenney, Karen Latchana. *Saving the American Bison (Great Animal Comebacks)*. Minneapolis: Jump! 2019.

Petrillo, Lisa. *All About North American Bison (Animals Around the World: North American Animals)*. Hallandale, FL: Mitchell Lane Publishers, 2019.

LEARN MORE ONLINE

1. Go to **www.factsurfer.com**
2. Enter **"Bison Comeback"** into the search box.
3. Click on the cover of this book to see a list of websites.